On The Nightstand

H.C Harper

BookLeaf Publishing

India | USA | UK

Presentation by *BookLeaf Publishing*

Web: www.bookleafpub.com

E-mail: info@bookleafpub.com

ISBN: 978-93-5744-320-3

First edition 2022

DEDICATION

I dedicate this book to my mom who has passed away who taught me my first love of writing and the importance of keeping a pen and paper near, you never know when an idea will strike.

I also dedicate this book to my husband who encourages me to work on my writing and my dreams and to all the rest of my family.

A Trip To Heaven

Today I took a trip to heaven, but only in my
mind.
I wanted to know what it's like to leave all you
love behind.
I drew a deep breath and closed my eyes to see
It was beautiful but how can I find thee?

It's so bright here, so much radiant light.
Everything so pearly white and bright.
I saw several angels passing by
Except only one of them caught my eye
You look exactly as you did here on earth
Except, maybe happier in your rebirth.
You noticed me staring your way
You smiled at me and this is what you had to say

"My sweet child, my daughter, it's not your time
yet.
God will call you home one day, but until then
don't forget
Even when she does, a mother's love never dies.
Only until we meet agains here no goodbyes.

"Please tell your sister that it wasn't her fault
To my husband say 'Righteousness exalts"

And remind your brother that he doesn't always
need to be strong
and for you my sweet girl, remember that you
belong"

With that she disappeared and the light too
I opened my eyes unsure of what else to do.
Was it all in my head or did it actually transpire?
But as I walk away, I hear the sounds of the
heavenly choir.

The Girl

Who is that girl? I do not know.
She is quite cheerful though.
Full of joy like a starry night
She swings and she sways with delight

She reminds me of me before,
Someone who I did adore.
Carefree and innocent, helping everyone she
could.
Without a pause to consider if she should.

I flash a smile as she looks my way.
and pause to consider what I should say.
Do I tell her she is going to get hurt?
That it's safer if she stays alert?

On second thought, I should keep quiet
Keep my thoughts and comments private.
I wish they never would have brought it up to
me
That way I could be like her, carefree.

Sincerely

Since the moment I saw you
I knew that you'd be mine
Never had a doubt with eyes so blue
Callin' you my valentine
Every day since we met
Red roses near your picture hung up on the wall
Every moment I won't forget
Listed here in my journal I have it all
Your favorite places, routine, shops and so much more.

You didn't notice me at first standing near the door
Or maybe you still haven't yet
Unable to tell to be quite honest
Really, I'm not any threat

Seeing you all riled up I'm at my calmest
Tomorrow is another day to try
Although I don't understand why we couldn't do tonight

Leaving you isn't easy to do but you understand
why

Knowing I'm here would be half of the fight
Except you'll never know until I decide
Remember, when your ready I'll be right outside

Eagle

Warming afforest
A black, fierce raven wallows
because of the claw

The Flamingo

so long
    rather silly
   ever so gorgeous
   decidedly charming
  dynamic, magic, fool
 beautiful, magic, hot
beautiful, magic, fool
rather living   silly!
very long   hearts
so pink   speaks
 alive   hearts
 morals   so long
  whoosh   Flamingo
   take   my people
     my friend
    I love you
    my mother   all charming
  cheerfully   dynamic, magic, open
  make money   beautiful, dynamic, fool
 quite long   tall leg skimming, suddenly
 the night   its long peg hopping, suddenly
my friend   eternal peg skittering, suddenly
very tall long-distance leg jumping, suddenly

its semipermanent wooden leg skimming, suddenly
perennial leg, physical strings, extant morality
 longstanding leg, active strings, realistic ethics
 perennial branch, nimble strings, realistic ethics
  tenacious stage, dynamic strings, absolute morality
  sesquipedalian leg, physical strings, extant morality
   tenacious stage, progressive strings, absolute ethics
    eternal branch, hot strings, realistic ethical motive
     its lifelong branch jumping, suddenly my people a
      long wooden leg jumping, suddenly gorgeous
          tall fork skimming, suddenly   pop
            beautiful, magic, agile
              magic, mean, fool
               ever so active
                very charming
                living tickle
                 heart whoosh
                 class   crazy
                 never   pink!
                 night   never
                 heart   never
                 night   whoosh

8

pink   living
long   all pink
heart very pink
rather living
very small
gorgeous
all pink
very pink
pink get
long and
about see
gotta and
get   man
time was
in   pop
was
got
end
got
could
make money
rather silly
my friend

The Pen & The Paper

My perfect pen, you inspire me to write.
How I love the way you mark, write and glide,
Helping me get my thoughts out this night,
Always writing and you help me do it with
pride.

Fierce winds shake the leafage of September,
And end autumntime has the trees cleared.
As the time passes the words help me remember.
Even at times if it's a little bit weird.

Oh but my journals help me too
Holding the secrets to the past
One day I'll be able to pass them on so others
can view
Frozen in time so that they last

On The Calm Black Water

In a dream I shall feel of dark blue velvety
jacket;
Pours burning love beautiful as snow;
That by starlight! He sings and the woods sing!

In the wine of daylight dark lilacs.
- its coolness on my feet, down the long black
river.
The wolves howl back on the delighted earth.
- from violet forests: where the stars are
sleeping.

How the earth is, on the calm black water
Snow of rose petals and the poet says
it was the voice but endless;

I cared nothing for all, I have seen maelstroms
eternal,
of the sea star-infused and to know the skies
the scented twilight, the twisted trees

Sweet Nothings

You are the keeper of my dreams,
The man who holds my heart.
When spring flowers bloom, our love is bold,
like a comets light.
When autumn leaves fall, our love is gold,
shining bright like a starry night.

In summertime, our love is innocent, and full of
grace.
In wintertime, our love is warm — like the fire
in the fireplace.
If skies are blue, our love is playful — two
people singing in the sun.
If thunder rolls our love is blessed, a refuge from
the dancing rain as one.
True love stories never have endings.

Inspiration Vs Depression

We are more than who we think we are.
We should stop thinking that
We can't make it happen
You must know

We can help save the world together
I would be lying to you if I said
The future is not in our reach
We can all make it if we try hard enough

It 's silly to think that
Dreams are just hopes, which we can never
make happen
Most of us are meant to be ordinary
Well, I don't believe that

And every action we take matters
They say we make a difference
Our lifetime is short and not within our control
But that hardly changes anything, don't forget

We have a heart and a soul
They tell us
We pray and cry
We live and we die

The truth is
We live for a reason
It is not apparent that
The world is cold and dark

One Last Hope

Say good night
For as the hour draws near, the shadow fades
One last hope
So it will be
Blood stained
Not a prayer
Forgiveness,
A burial shroud on the table, a maroon soul
There is only embarrassment
A flickering candle on the table, next to a bible
There is only confusion
What happen? Why am I here?

The Next Generation

We live for the next generation.
We will not stop until we find a way to make
this dream come true.
They need to have a good foundation
And that starts with you

We live for the next generation.
We will encourage their hopes
Teach them morals and give them a good
education.
All while showing them the ropes.

We will fight for them, and we will fight for it
all again.
But we need to start now
If we don't start now, then when?
I know you agree, but are wondering how?

Break the generational chains
Plant a tree, pick up trash and teach them about
things they need to know.
When you are gone they will be all that remains,
So teach them well before you go.

You Gotta Stay

"You gotta stay"
And my old man got sick of it
And he's back at night, it's cold and he's drunk as
a beer
He said "I can't stay here, can't promise, can't
commit"
"You'll understand one day if you stay here"
And I said it "It isn't a sin to be
With a crowd of one or two
You know we can work it out just wait and see
You just gotta look inside you"

He never understood, never figured it out before
walking out the door
We get older, we change, we grow
Occasional hello and Merry Christmas but
nothing more
I used to beg you to stay but now you can just
go.

Laughing in the ashes

The people who are trying to turn their backs
Say they never lived here or would
There's nothing much enough to get us back to
where we started
These were people in my neighborhood

Making deals on dead end parts
For someone to turn to and find
At least one drop out who had the smarts
Did something stupid but was nothing but kind

Someone else who was afraid
Afraid someone is coming over
And he's looking at you
While the deals get made
And the cards are drawn
Looking for those shiny wheels and back alley
deals.

And those tables in the corner, nobody see's
them in this town
The guys tearin' hearts out when they come
around
And turning the world upside down
And laying the bones for burnin' out the ground

They think they're so cool
And laughing till they're covered in the ashes
And laughing laughing laughing laughing
laughing at the winners

The Troubles of Today

I'm thankful for the man who is happy
In spite of life's troubles this day. For him I pray
And the girl who sings for brighter tomorrow's
Because of the clouds and rain of today.

They didn't know they taught me so many things
To them they were just singing and cheerful
But we never know what tomorrow brings
We must greet it with a smile and not enter it
fearful.

The King & I

King rules eternally
Wait for me on both sides
Blood spills far away

Fight Like A Girl

Why is it in this day in age,
That a woman still has to fight for an equal
wage?
Don't get me started on a woman's own body
being an issue for politics
But we can't just wait for the day where for
everyone it clicks

Can't quite go back to burning bras either.
But I don't wanna listen to the misogynistic old
man neither.
Talking about how he didn't want 'no female
doctor'
Like they couldn't do their jobs right, and he was
better than her.

We've come a long way, but there's still much to
do.
Guys don't skip over this poem it applies to you
too.
Because it affects your mothers, daughters,
sisters and wives.
Are you going to let someone else tell them how
to lead their lives?

The City & A Cigarette

This city is a cold skyscraper I'll admit
Never grab a door.
You don't know what's behind it.
If you go in you might end up on the floor.

It's freezing the snow is falling strong.
Light up a cigarette so you can't see your breath.
All the things that end up happening here are
wrong.
The cities filled with smoke and death.

Take a drag and watch the flames that I can see.
This isn't a place meant for people like you, the
faint of heart.
I wonder what your therapist knows about me.
Get out now before this place rips you apart.

Love

Unrequited, unselfish
Cherishing, sweetly, admiring
It will always be this way
Devotion

Change

25

You never hear the garden grow
Or see the air we breathe
We simply know that it is there though
We feel it and we believe.

Flowers don't deny the rain
To clear the dead petals away.
Nor does night spurn the sun
When it's time for it to be day.

Things are in a constant state of change
So too must we be
Even though at times seem a little strange
Change can be good, you will see.

The Scales

I feel the scales tipping again and I,
I've weighed the alternatives this is a punishment
Justice , peace and harmony is the end goal.
I can clearly see both sides of the argument.

A natural born diplomat, a mediator as a whole.
Always tactful and concerned with equality
It really is my best quality
But also the worst that I have too
If you can't understand let me explain it to you.

It makes it really hard for me to decide on
anything unrehearsed.
I also consider myself more of an after thought
Making sure everyone else is taken care of first
Without really considering the trouble that
brought.

My Sister's Keeper

Am I my sister's keeper?
Or is she mine?
I keep her secrets
But we didn't always get along fine

We fought and we cried
Cussed each other out and
Even sometimes lied
But when pust came to shove we were by each
other's side.

A shoulder to cry on
An ear to listen
Covering for each other when our parents were
gone
And even sometimes a little too much wine in
the ktichen

So yes, I am my sister's keeper,
And yes, she's also mine
Fierce friends and a bond a lot deeper.
Until the end of time.